The Art of Dispute Resolution
Tactics to Achieve Mutual Gain

Cedric Donald Owens

Table of Contents

1. Introduction 2
2. Understanding Conflicts: The Fundamentals 3
    2.1. The Nature of Conflicts 3
    2.2. The Anatomy of Conflicts 3
    2.3. The Life Cycle of Conflicts 4
    2.4. The Impact of Conflicts 5
    2.5. In A Nutshell 5
3. Diving Deeper: Unpacking the Psychology of Disputes 6
    3.1. The Human Predisposition: Understanding Disputive Behavior from an Evolutionary Perspective 6
    3.2. The Cognitive Aspect: Perceptions, Beliefs, and Cognitive Biases 7
    3.3. Emotions and Conflict: The Double-edged Swords 7
    3.4. The Role of Communication: Non-verbal Cues and Conflict 8
    3.5. Personalities and Conflicts: Navigating the High seas of Disputes 8
    3.6. The Social context of Conflict 8
4. The Zen of Listening: Opening Doors towards Communication 10
    4.1. Understanding Listening: Beyond Hearing 10
    4.2. Active Listening: Cultivating Engagement 11
    4.3. The Power of Silence 11
    4.4. Paraphrasing and Perceptual Checking 12
    4.5. Empathetic Listening: Feeling with the Speaker 12
    4.6. Wrapping it Up: Building Bridges 13
5. Empathy's Role: Acknowledge Differences and Find Common Ground 14
    5.1. Empathy: The Unseen Bridge 14
    5.2. Acknowledging Differences: Breaking Down Barriers 15

    5.3. The Magic of Common Ground 15
    5.4. Cultivating Empathy: The Practical Steps 16
    5.5. Leveraging Empathy in Conflict Resolution 16
6. The Power of Dialogue: Turning Disputes into Conversations 18
    6.1. Embracing the Power of Constructive Dialogue 18
    6.2. Steps into the Landscape of Dialogue 18
    6.3. Techniques Supporting the Dialogue Process 19
    6.4. When Dialogue Turns Chaotic 20
    6.5. The Power of Silence in Dialogue 20
7. Negotiation: The Art and Science of Reaching Agreements 21
    7.1. Understanding the Concept of Negotiation 21
    7.2. Identifying the Types of Negotiative Processes 22
    7.3. Unveiling the Principles of Effective Negotiation 22
    7.4. Exploring Handy Negotiation Techniques 23
    7.5. Mastering the Art of Negotiation 23
8. Creative Problem Solving: Transform Hot Buttons into Cool Comforts 25
    8.1. Creative Problem-Solving: An Introduction 25
    8.2. The Four-Step Model for Creative Problem-Solving 26
    8.3. Benefiting from Creative Problem-Solving 27
    8.4. Implementing Creative Problem-Solving in Our Everyday Lives 27
9. Aim for Win-Win: Strategies to Achieve Mutual Gain 29
    9.1. The DNA of a Win-Win Situation 29
    9.2. Building Toward a Win-Win Scenario 29
    9.3. Tools for Crafting a Win-Win Solution 30
    9.4. Cautionary Measures in a Win-Win Approach 31
    9.5. Extra Miles Towards Sustained Success 31
10. Staying Miles Ahead: Preventing Conflicts before They Arise 33
    10.1. The Foresight Factor 33

    10.2. Building Preventive Communication 34

    10.3. Establishing Norms and Policies 34

    10.4. Nurturing an Inclusive Environment 35

    10.5. Proactive Dispute Resolution Skills 35

11. Solidifying the Gain: Maintaining Resilience and Relationships in the Face of Future Conflicts 37

    11.1. The Importance of Conflict Consolidation 37

    11.2. The Role of Resilience in Maintaining Peace 38

    11.3. Investing in Relationships 38

    11.4. Strategies to Prevent Future Conflicts 38

    11.5. Building Resilience for Future Challenges 39

    11.6. Maintaining the Gain 39

Peace is not absence of conflict, it is the ability to handle conflict by peaceful means.

— Ronald Reagan

Chapter 1. Introduction

Unlock the secrets to mastering conflict resolution with our Special Report: "The Art of Dispute Resolution: Tactics to Achieve Mutual Gain." This enlightening guide isn't just about dull theory or technical tactics, but a vibrant journey of personal growth and professional betterment. It is infused with actionable strategies and real-life examples, bringing a refreshing perspective to a critical but often ignored skill set. Whether you're dealing with a cranky colleague, tough business negotiations, or even everyday interpersonal hurdles, this report is your golden ticket to transforming conflict into cooperation, friction into fulfilment, disputes into gains. Don't just resolve conflicts—redefine them! Break free from the chains of discord and embrace a thriving atmosphere of harmony and mutual success. Invest in your future today because peace isn't just beautiful, it's undoubtedly profitable.

Chapter 2. Understanding Conflicts: The Fundamentals

Our journey towards mastering conflict resolution begins at the very roots, understanding what conflicts truly are. A conflict, in its most basic definition, is a disagreement or discord that arises when two or more parties perceive incompatible goals, interests, actions, ideas, or values. But it's essentially so much more than that.

2.1. The Nature of Conflicts

Conflicts are an inherent part of human existence. They manifest in various forms and frequencies, from minor disagreements between friends, to tacit tensions at the workplace, to large-scale wars between nations. It is almost impossible to imagine a world without conflicts because they are intrinsically woven into our social fabric.

Conflicts serve an important function—they present an opportunity for growth, for change, for improved dialogue, and for better relationships. They are not inherently bad or good, but merely a powerful signal that something needs to change. The outcome of conflicts depends on how we handle them, and this, in turn, is heavily influenced by our understanding of their nature.

2.2. The Anatomy of Conflicts

Though conflicts emerge from a plethora of circumstances and personality dynamics, at the heart of every conflict lie two key elements:

1. Divergency of Interests: Conflicts often arise from varying needs, wants and interests. These can range from tangible resources (like money, time, and space) to intangible interests like

recognition, security, and love.

2. Perceived Threat: Conflicts take root and grow in potency when parties perceive threats to their interests—real or imagined. The intensity of a conflict directly relates to the perceived size and nature of the threat.

Understanding these components allows us to take a more empathetic and analytical approach to conflict management.

2.3. The Life Cycle of Conflicts

Conflicts aren't constants; they flow and evolve, increasing or decreasing in intensity, morphing continuously. Understanding this life cycle can enhance our skills in conflict resolution. Here's the general life cycle of conflicts:

1. Latent Conflict: During this phase, the conflicting interests exist, but the parties may not be entirely aware of them.
2. Emergence: In this phase, parties become aware of the conflict and tensions start to build.
3. Escalation: If unaddressed, the conflict escalates, leading to increased tension and hardening of positions.
4. Stalemate: This is the most challenging phase of a conflict, where reaching an agreement becomes seemingly impossible.
5. De-escalation/Negotiation: With proper negotiation tactics, the conflict de-escalates.
6. Settlement/Resolution: The parties reach an agreement, resolving the conflict.
7. Post-Conflict Cooperation: The parties implement the agreement, paving the way for cooperation and relationship repair.

Being cognizant of these stages can help us shape our strategies and take actions at the right time to prevent conflicts from leading to undesirable outcomes.

2.4. The Impact of Conflicts

Understanding conflicts is incomplete without recognizing their impacts which are two-pronged: they can have destructive effects or constructive outcomes.

On the destructive side, conflicts can lead to stress, resentment, hostility, injustice, violence, and even war. They can deteriorate relationships and build walls of misunderstanding between people.

Conversely, when managed well, conflicts can lead to greater understanding, healthier relationships, effective change, and enhanced creativity. They force us to look at problems from different angles, pushing us out of our comfort zones, in turn fostering resilience and adaptation.

2.5. In A Nutshell

Conflicts are not as ominous as they seem – they are simply a call for change, for dialogue, and for understanding. Recognizing this simple truth is the first step towards becoming skilled at conflict resolution. As we journey ahead, we will delve deeper into the psychology of disputes, the role of effective communication, the power of empathy, and a treasure trove of practical strategies that harness the power of conflicts for mutual gain and sustainable peace.

Remember, the key to resolving conflicts doesn't lie in evading them, but in understanding and embracing them as catalysts for growth and improvement. As we get better at working with our conflicts, we'll witness how they transform from a sources of stress to opportunities for individual and collective growth. So, buckle up and prepare yourself for a deep dive into the fascinating world of dispute resolution.

Chapter 3. Diving Deeper: Unpacking the Psychology of Disputes

Welcome to a cerebral adventure as we attempt to intertwine conceptual threads from numerous schools of thought to unveil a comprehensive understanding of the psychology behind disputes. This chapter delves into the human psyche, revealing the inherent predispositions, cognitive mechanisms, and emotional impulses that play crucial roles in the development and escalation, as well as the resolution of conflicts. By scrutinizing psychological principles, our objective is to heighten your aptitude for assessing the central aspects of disputes, thereby equipping you with the necessary tools for effective conflict resolution.

3.1. The Human Predisposition: Understanding Disputive Behavior from an Evolutionary Perspective

Venturing back into the annals of human evolution, conflict traces back to our primal need for survival. Our Paleolithic ancestors who were better at requisitioning resources via competition, overt or covert, realized superior survival and procreation chances. Hence, some level of dispositional aggressiveness and capacity for disputes got ingrained in our genetic makeup. Today, the confluence of these instinctual imprints and environmental stimuli manifests in disagreements and conflicts evident in all walks of life. The relics of our survival-oriented past thus provide indispensable insight into our inherent predisposition towards disputes.

3.2. The Cognitive Aspect: Perceptions, Beliefs, and Cognitive Biases

Cognitive psychology brings forth another piece of the puzzle by shedding light on the role of individual perceptions, beliefs, and cognitive biases in conflicts. When disputing parties possess conflicting beliefs, misinterpret intentions, or harbor problematic biases, paving the path to a dispute becomes almost inevitable. A prime example here is the 'fundamental attribution error' which leads individuals to over-attribute others' behavior to their personality traits while downplaying situational influences, leading to perception gaps and escalating disputes. Familiarizing oneself with these biases can help in being vigilant, thereby minimizing their impact on conflicts.

3.3. Emotions and Conflict: The Double-edged Swords

Emotions play an intricate role in the occurrence and management of disputes. They can act as double-edged swords, either driving us into the tumultuous pit of disagreements or guiding us towards resolutions. A nuanced understanding of emotion cultivation, regulation, and expression can vastly aid in refining one's dispute resolution toolbox. Feelings such as anger can escalate conflicts, whereas other emotions like empathy and remorse can help mitigate them. The key lies in identifying the appropriate emotions to steer towards dialogue and resolution, and away from destructive conflict.

3.4. The Role of Communication: Non-verbal Cues and Conflict

In essence, disputes are a symptom of flawed communication. Non-verbal communication plays a significant role in this sphere. Reliance on facial expressions, body language, and tone of voice can often lead to interpretation errors and exacerbate conflicts. Great communicators are adept at reading these cues and adjusting their responses to diffuse potential conflicts. They utilize active listening skills as a powerful tool for conflict resolution.

3.5. Personalities and Conflicts: Navigating the High seas of Disputes

Another insightful angle taps into the realm of personality psychology. Different personality traits contribute uniquely to how we respond to disagreements. Highly neurotic individuals might have higher tendencies for conflict engagement, whereas agreeable people might try and avoid disputes, potentially leading to unresolved feelings. Recognizing individual personalities can significantly aid in customizing conflict resolution strategies for more effective outcomes.

3.6. The Social context of Conflict

Last but not least, social psychology unravels the influence of group dynamics and social context on disputes. Phenomena like social conformity and group polarization can escalate conflicts within and between groups. Emphasizing shared identities and common goals can help alleviate tensions and promote a collaborative resolution.

What you've embarked upon in this chapter will aid you in discerning the diverse psychological intricacies woven into the fabric of disputes. By comprehending these facets, you are well on your way towards utilizing the power of psychological understanding to convert potentially disruptive conflict scenarios into conduits of mutual growth and prosperity. Our evolutionary past, cognitive mechanisms, emotional responses, communication abilities, personality characteristics, and social influences collectively chart the course of disputes and their resolution. Harness these learnings effectively, and your journey towards mastering the art of dispute resolution will become intriguingly insightful and remarkably rewarding.

Chapter 4. The Zen of Listening: Opening Doors towards Communication

In the vast universe of dispute resolution, one practice stands out for its simplicity and power: The art of listening. This chapter will explore the depth and breadth of this essential facet of effective communication, illuminating the steps and strategies that can transform listening from a passive act into an active process of understanding, empathy, and ultimately, resolution. From theoretical insights to practical applications, this dive into the Zen of Listening will redefine your understanding of one of the most overlooked aspects of conflict resolution.

4.1. Understanding Listening: Beyond Hearing

Listening, in the context of dispute resolution, extends far beyond the biological act of hearing. It reaches into the realms of empathy, understanding, and connection. Hearing represents a physical process, wherein sound waves are captured and interpreted by the brain. On the other hand, listening is a more nuanced, subjective act of intentional focus and understanding. As Stephen R. Covey, author of 'The 7 Habits of Highly Effective People,' so aptly put it, "Most people do not listen with the intent to understand; they listen with the intent to reply."

Listening is also intrinsically related to the concept of 'presence.' To cite the mindfulness teachings from Eastern philosophy, being present means bringing your consciousness and attention fully into the here and now without judgment. This sets the stage for active listening, fostering an environment that encourages mutual understanding, empathy, and constructive discourse.

4.2. Active Listening: Cultivating Engagement

Active listening is a critical tool for effective communication and conflict resolution. It involves mindful attention and engagement with the speaker—physically, verbally, and non-verbally—demonstrating a sincere interest in their words and feelings to foster open, honest dialogue.

Implementing active listening can look like many things. It may entail verbal affirmations such as "I hear you," or "I understand," alongside non-verbal cues, such as nodding or maintaining eye contact. It may also include paraphrasing or summarizing the speaker's points to ensure comprehension.

Active listening prevents misconceptions, reinforces shared understanding, and creates a secure environment where all parties feel valued and heard. These outcomes serve as the foundation for effective conflict resolution.

4.3. The Power of Silence

Amid the flurry of conversation, silence is a potent tool often underutilized. It allows space for thought, reflection, and absorption of the spoken word. Giving the speaker space to formulate and express their thoughts without interference or interruption compels them to delve deeper into their feelings and perspectives, often resulting in more profound, honest communication.

Used wisely, silence can be a catalyst for open dialogue and a powerful means to unearth underlying issues, making it an indispensable part of the listener's toolkit.

4.4. Paraphrasing and Perceptual Checking

Paraphrasing and perceptual checking are vital active listening strategies that foster clear, effective communication.

Paraphrasing involves repeating the speaker's words in your own language. Doing so ensures the listener's understanding of the issue at hand and gives the speaker a chance to clarify if needed.

Perceptual checking takes this one step further by allowing the listener to validate their understanding.

A perceptual check could sound like, "So what I heard you saying is..." or "It sounds like you're feeling..." This approach offers the speaker a chance to affirm the listener's understanding or correct misunderstandings, ensuring both parties are on the same page.

4.5. Empathetic Listening: Feeling with the Speaker

Empathetic listening goes beyond the comprehension of words to engage with the emotional subtext of the speaker's message. Such empathetic engagement allows the listener to "step into the shoes" of the speaker and encourages a deeper, more holistic understanding of their feelings and perspectives.

By expressing empathy towards the speaker's emotions, listeners can foster a sense of validation and acknowledgment, which often goes a long way in consolidating trust and bridging gaps in communication.

4.6. Wrapping it Up: Building Bridges

The Zen of Listening involves the understanding that listening is not a passive act—we listen to understand, to empathize, and to build bridges. The act of listening is potent; it can validate feelings, build trust, clarify misunderstandings, and foster a conducive environment for constructive dialogue and conflict resolution.

By applying these theoretical insights and practical strategies, you can transform your listening experience into a journey towards mutual understanding, empathy, and ultimately, resolution.

In the next chapter, we delve into 'Empathy's Role: Acknowledge Differences and Find Common Ground,' where we further explore the power of empathetic connection in dispute resolution. Until then, indulge in the Art of Listening. Remember, the door to resolution might just lie in lending a patient, empathetic ear.

Chapter 5. Empathy's Role: Acknowledge Differences and Find Common Ground

In the grand theatre of conflict resolution, various actors play their parts in driving the narrative forward, and one of the most understated yet pivotal characters is that of empathy. The dance of empathy is not just about understanding another's feelings, but also acknowledging their differences and seeking out the common ground where seeds of resolution can take root and blossom. This chapter greets you with an exploration of empathy's role in conflict resolution—a journey that not only discerns the power of acknowledging differences but also celebrates the beauty of finding commonality amidst diversity.

5.1. Empathy: The Unseen Bridge

Empathy is akin to an unseen bridge that enables a person to travel across the chasm of misunderstanding and reach the shores of another's perspective. It is more than just feeling for another—it's about feeling with them, immersing oneself in their encompassing narrative, and glimpsing the world through their eyes. When one comes face to face with conflict, empathy helps view this landscape from the opponent's vantage point, unraveling valuable insights about their motivations, fears, and pain points.

A healthy sense of empathy necessitates the delicate balance of cognitive and emotional aspects. Cognitive empathy lets one comprehend another's thought process, often instrumental in intellectual debates and negotiations. Conversely, emotional empathy allows us to genuinely feel the emotional distress reverberating from the other party—a tool that is indispensable in personal and emotionally charged conflicts.

5.2. Acknowledging Differences: Breaking Down Barriers

Acknowledging differences, contrary to popular belief, does not cultivate division but is the cornerstone for shaping empathy. It is by understanding and acknowledging these differences that we can dismantle barriers and foster understanding.

When we encounter someone whose perspective clashes with ours, our intrinsic bias might lead us to brand their viewpoint as 'wrong' or 'misguided'. Yet, empathy nudges us to resist this reflex. Rather than judging, assume a learning perspective, observing these differences as a way to expand our understanding. Differences in opinions are not fissures; they are opportunities designed to enrich our personal growth and widen our perspective.

5.3. The Magic of Common Ground

Discovering common ground in a thunderous cloud of disagreement is not an easy feat, yet it is where the magic occurs. When empathizing, we don't just search for differences and parallels in thoughts—we seek to uncover shared values, beliefs, or concerns, no matter how seemingly minute.

Finding mutual areas of concern or shared objectives can steer contentious conversations towards the realm of collaboration. Toggling the focus from contentious points to shared interests can turn a dispute into a problem-solving expedition—a quest where opposing parties come together to tackle a common foe.

5.4. Cultivating Empathy: The Practical Steps

However, empathy is not a switch that can be effortlessly flicked on. It is a skill that demands deliberate cultivation and practice. Listen attentively, not just to the words but to the emotions behind them. Pay attention to non-verbal cues—body language, tone of voice—as they are often a wharf where unspoken sentiments dock. Validate their feelings and perspective, even if you don't agree. Validation is not about accepting but understanding.

Don't interrupt or rush to insert your viewpoint. Let them feel seen, heard, and appreciated. Use reflective statements like "It sounds like you think...," or "I understand you're feeling this because...". Practice patience and resist the temptation to jump to quick solutions. Often, it's not about providing an answer but creating space for them to unveil their solution. The aim is not to win a disagreement, but to cement understanding and cultivate connection.

5.5. Leveraging Empathy in Conflict Resolution

Applying empathy in conflict resolution is like employing a master key—it unlocks doors towards understanding, trust, and collaboration that were previously inaccessible. It has the power to shift the narrative, to take the dialogue from "you vs. me" to "us vs. the problem."

Moreover, parties tend to reciprocate empathetic demeanors—generating a positive feedback loop of understanding and recognition, which fosters mutual respect. Empathy has a domino effect that can turn a room thick with conflict into a stage where cooperation and concord can thrive.

In conclusion, empathy is not a panacea for all discords. Still, it is an invaluable tool that arms you with a deeper understanding of the landscape of disagreements and refines your journey towards peace. Merely perceiving it as a reconciliation tool undervalues its profound potential — Use it not just to resolve discords, but to reconstruct them in a harmony, appreciate diversity, and build connections, and let the symphony of understanding orchestrate an environment of mutual growth and gain.

Chapter 6. The Power of Dialogue: Turning Disputes into Conversations

A skilful dialogue enables us to transform the daunting disputes that arise between individuals or groups into more constructive and relationship-building conversations. This chapter will delve into the practical nuances of utilizing dialogue in conflict resolution, mapping the landscape of the dialogue process, and offering elaborate strategies to create space for effective communication.

6.1. Embracing the Power of Constructive Dialogue

Suppose a dispute can be considered as a hefty, immovable stone. In this context, dialogue serves as the chisel and hammer, breaking down the seemingly insurmountable barriers of conflict to pave a path to resolution. This is because dialogue operates on a premise of reciprocity, where each party feels as though they are heard and understood by the other. The crux is to transform binary oppositions into collaborative exchanges. Here, dialogue does not just concentrate on addressing conflicts, but also aims at fostering understanding, generating new insights, and forging meaningful relationships.

6.2. Steps into the Landscape of Dialogue

Engaging in dialogue commences with a leap of faith, an openness towards acknowledging diverse perspectives and an agile attitude to adapt accordingly. To bring about a profound change, follow these steps:

- Preparing for Dialogue: Set the right mindset. Inculcate an adaptive mental model that is open to learning rather than rigidly adhering to preconceived notions.
- Initiating Dialogue: The first touchpoint of communication is often critical. Craft this cautiously by focusing on expressing opinions with respect and openness.
- Maintaining Dialogue: Cultivate a pattern of listening actively, asking questions, and acknowledging the feelings and perspectives of the other person.
- Concluding Dialogue: Aim for a closure where both parties feel understood, even if the dispute has not been completely resolved.

6.3. Techniques Supporting the Dialogue Process

Understanding and efficiently applying certain techniques can accelerate, streamline and enhance the dialogue process significantly. Among these, we shed light on the most effective ones below:

- Active Listening: This implies listening with all senses, not just to comprehend the words spoken, but to catch the underlying emotions, and the unspoken messages as well.
- Balanced Advocacy and Inquiry: Striking the right balance between stating one's viewpoints (advocacy) and asking questions to understand the other (inquiry) can prevent the conversation from becoming one-sided or unproductive.
- Building a "Golden Bridge": It's a term coined by negotiation expert William Ury. To build a "Golden Bridge," offer a solution that meets the interests of both parties, and helps the other party save face, it ensures more collaborative communication.

- Mindful Responding: Instead of reactive responses, opt for mindful responses. This implies processing information, reframing it positively if needed, and then delivering a response.

6.4. When Dialogue Turns Chaotic

At times, even the best initiated dialogues can turn chaotic due to emotional outbursts, misunderstandings, or slipping prejudices. In such scenarios, remember, the goal is to steer the conversation back to a more productive state. This could be accomplished by giving space for letting out emotions, scheduling another session to avoid fatigue-led disagreements, and apologizing if you realize any inappropriate remarks from your end.

6.5. The Power of Silence in Dialogue

Remember that in the multitude of words, lies chaos; in silence, lies clarity. Silence induces the participants to contemplate, assimilate, introspect, and then speak. It creates a cocoon of calmness, making the dialogue more transparent and significant.

In conclusion, dialogue is indeed a transformational tool in conflict resolution. A tool that requires understanding, empathy, patience, practise, and much tacit knowledge to wield efficiently. Yet, when utilised skillfully, dialogue has the prowess to turn contentious disputes into engaging conversations, sowing seeds for constructive, harmonious relations in professional and personal spheres alike.

Chapter 7. Negotiation: The Art and Science of Reaching Agreements

Negotiation, an intriguing amalgam of art and science, is the fulcrum upon which the resolution of conflicts teeters. It presides over the complex dance of appeasement, assertion, and persuasion, paving the path towards conciliation. To dissect this capacious subject, we shall progress along an avenue marked by five consequential milestones: understanding the concept of negotiation, identifying the types of negotiation, unveiling the principles of effective negotiation, exploring handy negotiation techniques, and, finally, unmasking the art of mastering negotiation.

7.1. Understanding the Concept of Negotiation

Negotiation refers to the interactive process wherein dissimilar parties strive for reaching mutually beneficial outcomes by making concessions and finding compromises. It revolves around the artistry of charisma, understanding, persuasion, and the hard science of strategies, principles, and techniques. This amalgamation of elements promotes effective communication, enhances relationships, and bolsters conflict resolution, leading towards a cooperative atmosphere.

The essence of negotiation is based on four core concepts: Needs, Rights, Power, and Relationships. Needs signify the parties' interconnected desires that could promote possible agreements. Rights embody the legal or ethical entitlements within the negotiation. Power represents the ability to influence the outcome through control or leverage. Lastly, Relationships encompass the interpersonal dynamics that influence interactions and decisions throughout the negotiation process.

7.2. Identifying the Types of Negotiative Processes

Negotiation embodies two primary modes: Distributive Negotiation and Integrative Negotiation.

- Distributive Negotiation, or 'zero-sum' negotiation, implies a situation where any gain to one party corresponds to a loss for the other. It operates on a scarcity mindset, asserting that resources are limited. This form is typified by aggressive tactics and self-interest.
- Integrative Negotiation, also known as 'win-win' negotiation, envisages a scenario where parties collaborate to expand resources or develop shared value. Inclined towards innovation and creative solutions, it ensuingly fortifies relationships, fosters trust, and facilitates mutual wins.

The two modes are not exclusionary, but rather, parties can switch between them depending upon resources, relationships, and desired outcomes.

7.3. Unveiling the Principles of Effective Negotiation

Three significant principles encapsulate the underpinnings of effective negotiation.

1. Preparation and Planning: The predilection to orchestrate beforehand provides a negotiator with detailed understanding, enabling judgement of possible outcomes, establishing goals,

strategies and also discerning the opponent's potential moves.

2. Open Communication: It involves building rapport, expressing needs clearly, and actively listening, fostering an environment of mutual respect and understanding.

3. Objectivity and Emotional Control: Negotiation often becomes heated, thus maintaining objectivity and emotional control helps in staying on track towards achieving desired outcomes, without derailing into unnecessary disputes.

7.4. Exploring Handy Negotiation Techniques

Several techniques assist in augmenting negotiation skills. The PIE method or Persuade, Influence, and Empower is one frequently used. 'Persuade' deals with logical arguments; 'Influence' encompasses emotional appeals, and 'Empower' fosters an environment where the other party feels validated, fostering an inclination towards mutual agreement.

'Reframing' allows negotiators to change the course of conversation by altering perspectives, ensuring better results. 'Mirroring' refers to subtly matching the other party's physical or verbal expressions, creating empathy and rapport.

7.5. Mastering the Art of Negotiation

Mastering negotiation involves continuous learning, practising, and adapting. This involves not only understanding the crux of negotiation but also elaborately studying one's self—the biases, strengths, weaknesses, and preferences.

Embracing empathy and cultivating patience, adopting active listening, persistently practising resilience, comprehensively preparing, and maintaining a fluid yet firm stance are some habits of efficient negotiators that can be nurtured over time.

In conclusion, negotiation is a paramount component of conflict resolution and general interpersonal dealings. From the realm of business boardrooms to domestic spheres, from political landscapes to the social arena, its presence persists ubiquitously. Adeptness at negotiation doesn't solely fetch you an advantageous deal or resolve a heated disagreement; it also catalyses the foundation of respectful relationships, fostering more harmonious environments where mutual benefit isn't a hopeful wish, but a tangible reality.

Chapter 8. Creative Problem Solving: Transform Hot Buttons into Cool Comforts

In our journey of conflict resolution and negotiation, we often approach situations where misunderstandings, disagreements, or contentious issues may feel like explosive hot buttons just waiting to be pushed. However, this chapter will guide you in transforming these potential conflicts into cool comforts using special techniques of creative problem-solving. These strategies will not only assist in hurdle-clearing by breaking down the walls of discord, but also in creating an environment conducive for better cooperation and understanding.

8.1. Creative Problem-Solving: An Introduction

The first significant step to transforming hot buttons into cool comforts is to understand what creative problem-solving means. It's a multi-step process that encourages us to challenge our preconceived ideas and conventional methods of doing things, to take a step back and broaden our perspectives, and to generate innovative solutions to conflicts – solutions that are satisfactory to all parties involved. This approach requires both analytical and creative elements with an aim to not only address the problem but to also build and maintain functional relationships between parties.

8.2. The Four-Step Model for Creative Problem-Solving

Creative problem-solving entails a structured four-step process, including clarifying and identifying the problem; generating ideas; developing and selecting solutions; and implementing the chosen solution.

1. Clarifying and Identifying the Problem

Conflicts often arise due to unclear understandings or misinterpretations. Hence, the first step of creative problem-solving involves identifying the problem clearly. This includes defining the situation, exploring all the reasons behind its occurrence, and understanding its nature and scope. Everyone involved must have a mutual understanding of what the problem is. As the old saying goes, 'A problem well stated is a problem half-solved.'

2. Generating Ideas

The next phase is the generation of as many ideas as possible to resolve the issue, often referred to as 'brainstorming.' It's essential to create a non-judgmental atmosphere that encourages free association and out-of-the-box thinking for all parties. The more ideas we generate, the greater the chance of finding a unique and acceptable solution.

3. Developing and Selecting Solutions

Once we have generated enough ideas, the next task is to sift through them, evaluating their practicality, feasibility, and acceptability. The goal is to narrow down the list to a few viable options, with each option having its potential pros and cons clearly evaluated. Parties involved should be comfortable with the selected solution that is balanced and fair.

4. Implementing the Chosen Solution

Finally, the agreed-upon solution needs to be implemented. This step involves creating an action plan, defining responsibilities for each party, and setting up mechanisms for monitoring progress. It's critical for the agreed solution to be delivered, ensuring a satisfactory outcome.

8.3. Benefiting from Creative Problem-Solving

Creative problem-solving adds significant value to the process of conflict resolution. By practicing this approach, we replace the heat of disagreement with the cool comfort of productive discussion. It also fosters positive relationships and goodwill among those involved. Recognising, understanding, and applying these techniques is a transformative process that allows us to change our perception of conflict. Rather than viewing conflict as an uncomfortable hot button issue, we learn to see it as an opportunity for creative problem-solving, growth, and improvement.

8.4. Implementing Creative Problem-Solving in Our Everyday Lives

Although this chapter specifically discusses creative problem-solving in the context of conflict management, its principles can be applied to almost any problem or challenge we face in our personal or professional lives. Whether it's resolving disagreements among team members, finding middle ground in a negotiation, or navigating through challenging family dynamics, creative problem-solving is an invaluable tool.

By integrating these methods into our regular thought processes, we begin to reshape our thinking patterns, and ultimately our conversations and relationships. This drastic shift in approach doesn't happen overnight, but with patience, practice, and willingness to change, transitioning from pushing hot buttons to fostering cool comforts can become second nature.

Remember, every conflict yields an opportunity for growth and creativity. By embracing creative problem-solving, we transform our approach, unlock new possibilities, and enhance our ability to handle conflicts. In doing so, we don't just resolve the dispute; we create a pathway to shared understanding, mutual respect, and enduring relationships.

Chapter 9. Aim for Win-Win: Strategies to Achieve Mutual Gain

To understand conflicts, we must first build a knowledge base of their origin, potential pathways, and abandonment schemes. Yet, mere comprehension is not enough. We must strive to harness the ecosystems of dialogue, negotiations, and creative problem solving to steer conflicts towards a reef of resolution. But, what if the golden resolution is one where everyone is a victor? Yes, we're talking about "win-win" solutions. Here's your comprehensive guide to manifesting them in real-life scenarios.

9.1. The DNA of a Win-Win Situation

At the heart of win-win strategies lies the fundamental belief that everyone involved in a conflict or argument can obtain a satisfactory outcome. This ethos is counter to the widespread notion that life is a zero-sum game, where one individual's gain often implies another's loss. Evidently, zero-sum thinking leads to competition, while win-win pushes for cooperation. Thus, aiming for a win-win situation promotes healthy interactions, ensures fair resolution of disputes, fosters better relationships among parties, and nurtures a positive environment.

9.2. Building Toward a Win-Win Scenario

The first step toward plotting a win-win outcome is understanding the other party's needs. Rather than focusing solely on your goal, analyze the fundamental objectives and interests of others. Utilize the skilled listening and empathy techniques you've cultivated from previous chapters. Remember that each dispute is a dialogue, and through genuine communication, you can unravel a broader perspective.

1. Let go of your assumptions: Resist the urge to judge the other party's intentions based on their reactions. Erroneous assumptions only create roadblocks in the path to resolution.
2. Seek first to understand, then to be understood: By making an effort to understand the other party's viewpoint before explaining yours, you foster trust and facilitate open dialogue.
3. Be open to change: In the pursuit of a mutual resolution, you may need to modify your perspectives or methods. Remain flexible.

9.3. Tools for Crafting a Win-Win Solution

How do you translate the blueprint of understanding needs into a concrete reality? The following tools might come in handy:

[] **Negotiation: A compelling conversation where you discuss, deliberate, and decide collaboratively.** [] Brainstorming: A creative exercise where both parties devise potential solutions without judgment. The wider the ideas, the more the chances of stumbling upon a win-win resolution. [*] Prioritization: Bring clarity by determining what's most important to each party. This action can help find commonalities and compromises.

Remember: the key to using these tools effectively is to maintain openness, foster empathy, and promote constructive dialogue.

9.4. Cautionary Measures in a Win-Win Approach

As with any process, the road to win-win comes with its pitfalls. Stay mindful of these:

1. Falling into a compromise trap: Don't hastily settle for an unfair compromise under the disguise of a win-win outcome. It creates unnecessary resentment otherwise avoidable with patience and dialogue.
2. Neglecting self-interest: While seeking a mutual solution, don't overlook your needs. Win-win is about mutual satisfaction—not self-sacrifice.
3. Confusing harmony for resolution: Temporary harmony should never be mistaken for a long-term resolution. Make sure the win-win solution addresses the root cause of the conflict.

9.5. Extra Miles Towards Sustained Success

The journey does not end at the creation of a win-win situation. To foster enduring results, you should continue engaging constructively, nurturing the relationship, and remaining open to altering strategies based on future developments—all whilst ensuring the inclusion of preventive measures against potential conflicts.

Through this chapter, we have aimed to provide an in-depth, detailed explanation of how to successfully implement and sustain a win-win approach in conflict resolution. By incorporating these practices, you will not just be resolving conflicts; you'll be transforming the very essence of disputes. As you continue to weave these strategies into your life, remember, the optimal outcome is not about one party overpowering the other. Instead, it's about achieving mutual satisfaction, a collective resolution where all parties feel accomplished—the real essence of winning.

Chapter 10. Staying Miles Ahead: Preventing Conflicts before They Arise

One of the central tenets of our report, "The Art of Dispute Resolution: Tactics to Achieve Mutual Gain," lies in not just incidentally stumbling upon resolution techniques when caught amidst disputes but in actively harnessing foresight to prevent conflicts from arising in the first place. This category of preemptive strategizing prompts us to consider the age-old dictum: 'prevention is better than cure.' However, how can one implement this in an environment teeming with differing opinions, backgrounds, interests, and emotions—each potential catalysts for a conflict? Let's delve deeper into this understanding.

10.1. The Foresight Factor

Foreseeing a conflict isn't about donning a fortune teller's hat and gazing into a crystal ball. Instead, it's about cultivating a perceptive and nuanced understanding of the social dynamics at play in any given environment. This requires a combination of empathy, insight, and observational analysis. We must sharpen our awareness to notice the shorthand communication, non-verbal cues, people's reactions, and the undercurrents of tension that could potentially evolve into a conflict. By spotting these signals early, it's possible to intervene and steer the situation away from conflict.

But how can we achieve this? Consider adopting a vigilant approach, like a meticulous gardener, who keenly observes the weather patterns, diagnoses the earth's quality, and intervenes in the plant's early life stages to circumvent foreseen adversities even before they manifest. Simultaneously, the gardener doesn't attach personal emotions to the weather or soil, avoiding unhealthy conflict with external factors. By transitioning to the role of an objective observer, it becomes easier to make rational and proactive decisions that could prevent a potential conflict.

10.2. Building Preventive Communication

To stop conflicts from emerging, effective communication is paramount. The focus here is two-fold: on the words chosen and attention to how these words are perceived. Every discourse we partake in holds the key to either fueling or diffusing potential tension in a situation. Hence, fostering habits like constructive criticism, active listening, and assertive communication can act as preventive agents.

Every conversation should aim to create a climate of openness, respect, and understanding. By mastering the art of being clear, concise, and coherent, disagreements borne out of misunderstandings can be side-stepped effectively.

10.3. Establishing Norms and Policies

Parallel to implementing individual efforts, organizational measures can be a powerful tool for mitigating conflicts proactively. This might involve drafting clear guidelines or communal norms that encourage positive interaction and discourage destructive behavior.

Policies should promote mutual respect, acknowledging diversity, and emphasizing active listening. Moreover, norms that foster an environment of emotional intelligence can provide a strong foundation for preventing conflicts.

10.4. Nurturing an Inclusive Environment

A culture of inclusivity and respect, where diversity is celebrated rather than suppressed, tends to be less prone to internal disputes. Encouraging an open-minded, empathetic, and accepting attitude fosters resilience against conflicts.

Thus, steps to foster inclusivity and celebrate diversity—whether it's through team-building exercises, workshops, or simply through the everyday examples set by the leaders of an organization—can lead to a harmonious environment capable of inhibiting conflicts before they bubble to the surface.

10.5. Proactive Dispute Resolution Skills

Developing proactive dispute resolution skills can be equated to frequently servicing a vehicle to ensure its smooth operation, rather than waiting for it to break down. Likewise, regular training sessions, workshops, and seminars on dispute management can arm individuals with the necessary skill set to manage and mitigate potential conflicts.

In wrapping up this exploration, we might consider that conflict isn't an unsolicited visitor but a consequence of an underlying issue—be it miscommunication, misunderstanding, or simply incompatible goals. Recognizing this allows us to swing the spotlight onto proactive strategies, addressing potential issues before they snowball into conflicts. Given that we've been trained to respond rather than prevent conflicts, adopting a preventive approach could feel like swimming upstream. But, with consistency, practice, and enhanced understanding, we can navigate our environment with an eye for prevention rather than cure. Remember, every step to preempt conflict is a step closer to a harmonious and productive coexistence.

Chapter 11. Solidifying the Gain: Maintaining Resilience and Relationships in the Face of Future Conflicts

Imagine having navigated the murky waters of conflict, zigzagging your way through difficult conversations and contentious issues, only to finally arrive at that coveted island of resolution. Undoubtedly, there's a deep sense of achievement. But the journey isn't over yet. In the aftermath of conflict, there are important tasks still to be addressed to ensure that the hard-won resolution lasts, to strengthen relationships and guard against the resurrection of the conflict or emergence of fresh disputes. This chapter, therefore, investigates the art of consolidating gains made through conflict resolution and methods for maintaining resilience and relationships amidst future discords.

11.1. The Importance of Conflict Consolidation

We must first understand why it is crucial to solidify the gains made through conflict resolution. Conflict consolidation is the process of reinforcing the solutions and agreements reached after a conflict-resolving process, to minimize the risk of the dispute resurfacing. It is a critical step that builds on the successful resolution of a dispute. By securing the gains made, you can turn past conflicts into strong foundations for future peace and productive collaborations. Doing this makes sure that the energy, time, and resources invested in settling disputes are not wasted, and that peace is preserved for the long haul.

11.2. The Role of Resilience in Maintaining Peace

Resilience refers to our ability to recover from setbacks and adapt to change, to keep advancing despite adversity. Strengthening personal and team resilience is a robust step towards curtailing the recurrence of conflicts. Building resilience involves cultivating emotional intelligence, improving stress management, promoting self-awareness, and fostering adaptability. Emotional intelligence ensures you can better understand your own and others' emotions, thereby preventing undue friction. Managing stress ensures you do not unknowingly trigger conflicts due to overwhelming pressure. Increased self-awareness promotes conscious communication, reducing the chances of misunderstandings, while adaptability ensures you can handle change and keep up with dynamic work environments, warding off potential conflicts.

11.3. Investing in Relationships

If buildings need strong pillars to be robust, relationships need transparency, respect, and communication to be sturdy. Post-conflict, investing time and effort into enhancing the relationship with your counterparts helps in future conflict resilience. Take the time to meet up with them, undertake joint activities, and build mutual trust and understanding. Acknowledge your differences and celebrate them. Highlight and appreciate the strengths of each side. This fosters mutual respect and wards off potential conflicts resulting from a lack of understanding or miscommunication.

11.4. Strategies to Prevent Future Conflicts

Many ties, conflicts arise as a result of miscommunication,

misunderstanding, or lack of transparency. Hence, clear, honest, and consistent communication is the best way to prevent potential conflicts. Develop strategies wherein everyone involved understands their roles, responsibilities, and the expectations from them. Also, lay down a blueprint for dealing with potential disputes so that no party feels taken aback when a conflict arises.

11.5. Building Resilience for Future Challenges

Resilience doesn't come overnight. It takes deliberate practice and patience. Start by acknowledging your past conflicts and learn from them. Identify what triggered them, how you responded, and whether your actions and words helped or escalated the situation. Use this knowledge as a stepping stone to strengthen your resilience. Find training programs or resources to develop necessary skills like patience, empathy, active listening, and critical thinking. These skills will ensure that when future conflicts arise, you are better equipped to handle them.

11.6. Maintaining the Gain

The essence of sustaining the gain ultimately boils down to the commitment of the involved parties towards peace. Be open to feedback and develop the habit of regular check-ins on how the implemented resolutions are working. If they are not working as anticipated, do not hesitate to revisit them. Remember, the goal is not just to resolve conflicts but to maintain the peaceful status quo in the face of future discrepancies or disagreements. Be proactive, be understanding, and above all, be patient.

So, there you have it. Conflict resolution doesn't end as soon as you've managed to put a stop to a particular discord. Instead, it continues, requiring you to continually nurture your relationships, build resilience, and anticipate potential conflicts. It compels you to not just solve the problem at hand but to prevent future ones. By understanding and mastering the art of 'Solidifying the Gain,' you'll ensure your peace is sustainable, relationships are productive, and future conflicts are prevented, or at least, minimized.

www.ingramcontent.com/pod-product-compliance
Lightning Source LLC
Chambersburg PA
CBHW070951220526
45471CB00007B/2984